T3-BUK-982

FINISHING LINE PRESS
www.finishinglinepress.com

Backyard Darwin

New and Found Haiku

poems by

Paul Stroble

Finishing Line Press
Georgetown, Kentucky

Backyard Darwin

New and Found Haiku

ISBN 978-1-63534-819-4 First Edition

ACKNOWLEDGMENTS

Many thanks to Dr. Tom Dukes, who encouraged this and previous projects and who made possible my dreams of writing poetry. I also thank Dr. Kim Kleinman, whose recommendation of Janet Browne's two-volume biography of Darwin opened my imagination; Dr. Charles Barnes, who also helped me tremendously on a previous project about religion and science; Dr. Nicole Miller-Struttmann, who read the project for accuracy; and Dr. Andrea Scarpino, whose poetry inspired me to experiment with longer forms. Many thanks also to Jane Ellen Ibur; Heather Derr-Smith; Maharat Rori Picker Neiss; the Webster Groves Starbucks; the Novel Neighbor Bookstore; the St. Louis Poetry Center; a wonderful family, Kris Lantz-Kaufman, Scott Kaufman, and Hailey Kaufman; and my dear friend Stacey Stachowicz and her family. My love is always for my family, Beth and Emily, and our crazy household with cats (*Felis catus*). Many thanks to Leah Maines and everyone at FLP.

I dedicate this poem to the memory of a wonderful science teacher and friend, Don Snyder.

Many of the haiku use words, passages, or ideas from the authors' texts or secondary sources, enough so to require citations. These haiku reflect my amateur reading of a variety of sources. I alone am responsible for any errors.

I worked on this poem over several months at my home in St. Louis, not in my backyard, although in my imagination I saw my childhood backyard in Vandalia, Illinois. After I thought of the title, I learned of and purchased a good book by James T. Costa, *Darwin's Backyard: How Small Experiments Led to a Big Theory* (New York: W. W. Norton, 2017), that not only discusses Darwin but also gives eighteen experiments that one can do at home.

Publisher: Leah Maines
Editor: Christen Kincaid
Cover Art: Joseph Wolf, Proceedings of the Zoological Society of London 1858
Author Photo: Jeannie Liautaud, Jeannie Liautaud Photography
Cover Design: Leah Huete

Printed in the USA on acid-free paper.
Order online: www.finishinglinepress.com
also available on amazon.com

Author inquiries and mail orders:
Finishing Line Press
P. O. Box 1626
Georgetown, Kentucky 40324
U. S. A.

Botanist Asa Gray (1810-1888), geologist Charles Lyell (1797-1875) with his wife Mary (1808-1873), naturalist Charles Darwin (1809-1882), and naturalist Alfred Russel Wallace (1823-1913) revolutionized science, knew each other, expressed appreciation for each other's work, and corresponded. Works of Carl Linnaeus (1707-1778), James Hutton (1726-1797), Jean-Baptiste Lamarck (1744-1829), Thomas Malthus (1766-1834), Étienne Saint-Hilaire (1772-1844), Louis Agassiz (1807-1873), Sir Joseph Dalton Hooker (1817-1911), Thomas Huxley (1825-1895), and the anonymous Vestiges of the Natural History of Creation *(1844) were discussed at the time, with Hooker, Huxley, and Agassiz active participants in scientific discussions. The research of Gregor Mendel (1822-1884) was not yet widely known. Stephen Jay Gould (1941-2002) and Richard Dawkins (born 1941) are among the many modern teachers of evolutionary science.*

I

Warm summer morning,
history, science, notebook.
Birds in our willow.

Picnic table, books
by Darwin, Wallace, Asa
Gray, Lyell. Iced Tea.

New axial age:
these colleagues, dedicating
books to each other.

Vaughan Williams' music.
Darwin was his great-uncle.
The lark ascending.

Among highest leaves,
our neighborhood mockingbird
sets a cheerful mood.

II

Lyell and Mary,
years of geological
research and travel.

Continental trips,
trips through the British Isles, and
two to the U.S.

Erosive action
of glaciers, Alpine basins,
glory of lakes, peaks.

Lake Geneva Rhone
erratics, glacial drift like
the Rhine's. Earth's long age.

Labyrinthodon
footprints in Pennsylvania
coal: an air breather.

Archaeopteryx,
wings like gallinaceous birds.
No feathered reptile.

Uncongenial
climate. Still, human fossils
in Forest Bed 3.

No human bones found
in the Somme alluvial
soil. (World War red zone.)

Virginia coal fields
in a granite depression
eastward of Richmond.

Fuller's earth, near Bath,
calcareous deposits,
fossil mollusca.

Age of copper lodes
close of the Silurian,
tin found near Wicklow.

Veins of copper, lead
in Wexford, Devonian,
later, in Cornwall.

Scottish glacial drift,
marine shells, mammoth remains,
Northumberland coast.

Pliocene strata
over half of Sicily
seen at Girgenti.

Central Asian loess,
what's called adobe in the
American West.

Loam of Brixham caves,
flint implements and bones of
ancient animals.

An ecology:
habitat and niche, "systems"
approach from Hutton.

Neptunism or
Plutonism, two theories
of rock formation.

Science and Bible:
fossils were left from older,
destroyed creations.

Catastrophism
nicely reflects Mosaic
creationism.

Now Lyell: the earth
was always as it is now,
and alters slowly,

a catastrophic
view to his peers: uniform
change over epochs.

Humans weigh the stars,
make lightning their slave. In form,
like the speechless brutes.

If humans were made
in God's image, then also
in the ape's image.

But to level us
with the brutes, omits reason,
morals, religion.

Divine origin
may be held beside theories
of transmutation.

Yet Linnaeus showed
us the similarities
of man and the apes....

Young Darwin, five years
on FitzRoy's *Beagle*, that long
journey set the stage

for all else he did,
and at sea he devoured
Lyell's *Principles*.

"Most all I have done
I owe to Lyell, dead, but
gone with mind intact."

III

Asa Gray, Harvard
botanist, unifier
of taxonomy

of American
plants—his botany books in
classrooms for decades—

studying flora
throughout the United States,
Europe, and Asia,

thorough lessons: names
of plants, seeds, growth, leaves, chapters
on morphology,

encouragement for
beginners learning genus,
species: persevere!

Learn from his passion:
38 years in search for
wild Oconee bells.

His landmark research,
the "Asa Gray Disjunction":
East Asian flora

identical to
flora native to our lands.
How did plants so spread?

It was the land bridge
across the Bering Strait, lost
in the next Ice Age.

His hypothesis
also confirmed Darwin and
challenged Agassiz—

ichthyologist,
geologist, founder of
glaciology,

but an advocate
of species fixity and
polygenism.

Hooker was Gray's friend,
a ground-breaking botanist
(no pun intended)

in his own right. Learn
from his passion, too: bio-
geographical

research in Britain,
India, Morocco and
Palestine, down to

Antarctica, up
to the Himalayas, and
the western U.S.!

Hooker, Gray, et al.
embraced empiricism.
Creationism

like Agassiz's, and
speculative ways like
Vestiges, were out.

Teleology
in natural selection?
Great thinkers quarreled.

And clear transitions?
We await more evidence
from fossil records.

Gray was convinced that
materialism need
not eliminate

religion. Look at
the religious, greatest minds,
Newton and Leibniz.

Agassiz's logic,
Darwin's empiricism:
science made that choice!

But Darwin sought not
the ultimate "why," only
the proximate "how."

Yet didn't Darwin
find satisfying answers
in nature's greatness,

and he shed belief
across his years? "Let each hope,
believe what he can."

IV

Wallace, explorer
of the Amazon and the
Malayan islands:

a major founder
of biogeography,
his demarcation

of flora, fauna
of Asia; on the east side,
of Australasia.

Still in print, his *Ma-
lay Archipelago,* since
1869,

influence upon
science, generations, and
writers like Conrad.

Insect, animal,
bird species, his collected
specimens gained from

14,000 miles
and eight years of voyages:
what discoveries!

Morning sun rises.
Orangs wake, feed in midday.
Dew long dried on leaves.

Islands of hot, moist
climate, thousands of species
he discovered there.

Ornithoptera,
the great birdwing butterfly
of north Maluku.

Bird of Paradise,
its species name *wallacei,*
from Bacan island.

Huxley, Wallace: did
birds descend from theropods?
Archaeopteryx

fossils Wallace found
suggest so. (Tonight I'll re-
watch *Jurassic Park.*)

The three large islands,
the peninsula: many
common mammals seen.

Remarkable are
colorations of insects,
birds of New Guinea.

Habitat species
emerge coterminous with
those closely allied.

Wallace: progression
of types of varieties
from an early type

indefinitely
continues, according to
the right conditions.

More diversity
in an area, ever
more diversity.

Animal structures,
external conditions, are
kept harmonious.

Two native wolves. One
with light form hunts deer, one with
bulky form kills sheep.

Titmice eat insects,
seeds, berries, grubs, depending
on their evolved bills.

Animals enjoy
their lives, entirely spared
fear of their own deaths.

The war of nature
is not incessant, no fear,
the healthy survive

as they adapt best
to their ecological
niche: nature's beauty.

How extinct species
are replaced with newer ones:
Wallace's question.

Wallace theorized
natural selection on
his own, apart from

Darwin, as he lay
sick with fever: inspired
by what he'd seen in

nature, and Malthus—
resources can't keep up with
population growth—

whom Darwin, Wallace
studied independently.
(Providence? Chance? Luck?)—

and ideas from
Vestiges of Creation,
Lamarck, Saint-Hilaire.

Vestiges: species
develop through orderly
laws found in nature.

Agassiz: species
are created in and for
their localities.

Even Lyell thought
species are immutable:
Wallace changed his mind.

Wallace emphasized
environmental pressures
on variations—

selection, like a
"centrifugal governor",
correcting defects,

irregular traits
keeping species adapting
in their habitats—

while Darwin focused
on competition among
members of species.

Darwin: females are
born with an aesthetic sense
for choosing their mates.

Not so for Wallace:
beauty is useful not just
for finding partners.

Is evolution
purpose driven? Wallace thought
so, Darwin did not.

Wallace's vision:
tropical life, life on worlds,
things of the spirit,

even land reform,
epidemiology,
glaciology,

ways humankind may
learn from their far siblings strange
to Western manners.

(At low stages of
society, we do find
perfect social states.

Our English "perfect"
society has crime and
poverty. Shameful!)

V

Backyard happiness:
when these facts and topics fit
the haiku pattern.

Fortunate haiku!
The Origin of Species,
seven syllables.

I count syllables
right-hand, *Sapiens* fingers,
thumbs evolved to grasp.

In 1950,
this *Origin* took a trip.
to Columbia.

The owner under-
lined passages, dripped sun tan
oil on Darwin's words.

1858:
announcement of what became
the paradigm shift:

selection explains
varieties of species:
Darwin and Wallace.

"There is a struggle
for existence leading to
the preservation

of profitable
derivations of structure
or instinct." Hard truth:

life, governed by death,
adaptation—not design.
"The death of Adam."

The balance may tip
so that a creature survives,
thus more progeny.

My new Pope couplet:
"God said, 'let *Darwin, Wallace*
be', and all was light."

Lyell, Hooker helped
establish priority
for Darwin's research.

Huxley called himself
"Darwin's bulldog", *Origin*'s
battling advocate.

Lyell, Huxley, Gray,
and Hooker pushed acceptance
of Darwin's theory:

odd friends otherwise
in their viewpoints, pursuits, and
personalities.

Hooker: selection
applies to botany, plant
geography, too.

Hooker gave Darwin
friendship and encouragement.
He was for Darwin

"the one living soul
from whom I have constantly
received sympathy."

Darwin gained the fame.
But take heart, Wallace! You're not
drawn as a monkey—

Darwin's ample beard,
eyebrows, enough like fur for
Punch caricature—

nor lend your name to
a "Wallace Award" for those
who "cleanse" our gene pool.

"If you hope to be
a naturalist, journey
to distant regions."

Forty-seven shells
on Galapagos beaches
are unknown elsewhere.

Amblyrhynelus,
a thick billed finch on its back,
share bits of cactus.

Finch with cracking bills,
finch that eat grubs: most famous
of Darwin's creatures:

don't they evidence
natural adaptation,
not divine design?

"One might fancy that,
from a paucity of birds
in this archipel-

ago, one species
has been taken, modified
for different ends."

"Not hopes, fears, but truth
as our reason permits us
to discover it."

"As our planet spins,
wonderful, endless life forms
are being evolved."

No one-hit wonder.
Darwin wrote twenty-four books
besides *Origin.*

"I cannot endure
doing nothing." D's careful
work let his mind sing.

Lyell's book in hand,
he theorized atoll and
coral formation,

the forms and structures,
fringing and distribution
of barrier reefs.

His work on orchids:
natural theology
in all but the name?

Hermaphrodite plants
now heterostyled, for cross
fertilization.

More vigorous plants
when cross-fertilized, become
more vigorous still.

Darwin feared that self-
fertilized plants would become
extinct. His own line?

Inevitably,
human descent must, too, be
traced to early forms.

"Sexual selec-
tion is the most efficient
among causes for

the differences
in external appearance
among man's races."

Wide-ranging thinker:
barnacles, orchids are each
hermaphroditic!

His favorite time in
his home countryside, peaceful
scientific lab.

Darwin found daily
peace among his potted plants.
Love of botany.

Darwin, Huxley watch
Drosera in the sunlight.
"Look, it is moving!"

Plants move on their own!
Darwin recast plant science,
a revolution.

Insect murder! The
sundew, its sticky leaves, most
sagacious plant.

Infants, suffering
even slight pain, close their eyes,
utter prolonged screams.

Eyelids firmly close,
the eyeball is protected from
being gorged with blood.

Upper lip draws up,
to keep mouth muscles wide, a
full volume of sound.

Yet no tears are shed,
lacrymal glands not yet formed,
our human weeping.

The insane may weep
long periods: memories,
or no cause at all.

Elephants weep, too,
suffering and tears when caged,
or the young removed.

Darwin: are inward
convictions of the divine
worthy evidence?

We personify
Nature, the total action
of natural laws

but need not claim that
God must rule through gravity
or say plants have will.

We expose living
things to new conditions. Now,
new variations.

The law of Lamarck.
Forms of life progress, higher
forms, higher purpose.

A question: what is
the mechanism by which
traits pass to offspring?

Too bad that Darwin
did not know about Mendel's
work on genetics,

but "Pangenesis"
was his provisional name
for what he observed.

Thanks to Mendel, we
know genetic change is first
individual.

Transmutation: no
longer understood in terms
of groups altering.

Spencer's classic phrase,
"survival of the fittest,"
improperly used:

genetic output,
not cut-throat economics
nor moral theory,

nor only fitness:
heritable qualities
are necessary,

and groups expand in
ecological niches
that have been empty.

Species transmutate
thanks to multiple factors.
No tautology.

Fisher, Haldane, Wright,
Dobzhansky helped advance the
modern synthesis.

VI

Origin, published
in America, looming
war between the states.

No more belief that
only whites were descendants
of Adam and Eve,

that racist theory.
Darwin helped American
abolitionists!

Lincoln the lawyer,
Darwin the biologist.
Both loathed slavery.

Who'd have thought Lincoln,
Darwin were born the same day?
A sign from God? No?

As much as Stonewall's
death, the country judged and bled
for an atonement.

Twenty seasons, dead
soldiers, white and black, ushered
into soil. Darwin:

ten tons of dry earth
pass through worms annually,
bury soil with soil.

Worm castings, dead leaves,
natural cultivation,
our thick rich humus.

Earth is reborn through
bodies of worms: Darwin's "new
creation story."

Didn't Lincoln, too,
think hard of death, that our lives
must end with the grave?

What of theistic
belief in the origin
of earth and its life?

Better to descend
from an ape, or from a man
of savage evil?

Church fathers demand
the literal agency:
Gen. 1 and 2:8.

Could not the Holy
Spirit have given Moses
accurate science?

Creation happened,
4004 BCE,
said Bishop Ussher.

Euclid's figures, proofs
traceable to Solomon,
even to Moses?

Huxley coined the word
"agnosticism," "follow
reason where it leads!"

Why do you complain
about Darwin's ideas?
They're in Lucretius

and Pythagorus:
the egg with the shell, growing
into perfect form.

Bible, not Darwin:
humans are the climax of
God's creative acts.

"Beloved is man
created in the image,
love made known to him"

The *Pirkei Avot*:
Ten utterances: the world,
and humans the crown.

Ten generations
from Adam down to Noah:
God's long-suffering.

All were created,
even things of the future
not recorded in

Scripture, by the First
Sabbath eve: manna, mitzvot,
rainbows. (Dinosaurs?)

The Sages: study
science, grow wise, do good works,
walk in ways of God.

Take Psalm 104:
humans are put into place
in Earth's systems, with

birds and beasts and fish,
"living things both small and great,
innumerable."

Faith ideally
seeks understanding: Nature,
and the revealed Word.

Human being: no
neurobiological
monism. *Nephesh.*

Spiritual truth:
we shall not all sleep in earth,
we shall all be changed.

We must not insist
that Genesis is science.
Faith's special beauty.

(Faith's other side: when
it's "lethally dangerous,"
our brutish nature.)

Wise the preacher who
learned, gave science updates to
his congregation.

Again, Darwin's praise:
"such grandeur, from so simple
a beginning, these

endless forms, most beau-
tiful, most wonderful, and
are being evolved."

Religion, science:
complementary knowledge.
Thank you, Dr. Gould!

Teach "alternatives"
to evolution theory
in public schools? No!

Don't confuse science
and religion! Email your
representative.

VII

Time to go in. Clouds.
Our species needs adventures,
yet shelter, safety.

Oh, our mockingbird!
How I'd fear you—if you were
still a theropod.

Consider life a
"voyage of discovery,"
favorite image.

Next week's vacation:
Grand Canyon's Vishnu base: Powell's
Unconformity.

How ancient the sand
for highway concrete? Our kicks
on Route 66.

How many fossils
heated, pressed to oil, refined
for millions of cars?

Going through Flagstaff,
I'll wave at, take a photo
of Agassiz Peak.

Charles and wife Emma,
children grown, veranda peace
in Kent countryside.

His mortal shell, not
in the churchyard, rather in
Westminster Abbey.

Ralph Vaughan Williams rests
nearby. May the lark and finch
ascend together.

“Happy is the one
that findeth wisdom and get-
teth understanding.”

Notes

Many of the haiku use words, passages, or ideas from the scientific texts or secondary sources, enough so to require citations. In the case of books that had several editions, I cite the editions that I used from my own collection.

Section I

"New axial age…" Among examples of friendly relations among these scientists: Darwin dedicated *A Naturalist's Voyage* to Lyell, and *The Different Forms of Flowers on Plants of the Same Species* to Gray; Wallace dedicated *The Malay Archipelago* to Darwin; Gray and Wallace wrote books and articles on themes of Darwin's theories; Darwin worked hard to successfully secure a government pension for Wallace in honor of the latter's scientific researches. Wallace also dedicated his book *Island Life* (1880) to botanist Joseph Dalton Hooker.

"Vaughan Williams' music…" Composer Ralph Vaughan Williams' maternal grandmother, Caroline Darwin Wedgwood, was Darwin's older sister, married to her cousin Josiah Wedgwood III, who was also the older brother of Darwin's wife Emma.

Section II

"Erosive action…" Sir Charles Lyell, *The Geological Evidences of the Antiquity of Man* (London: John Murray, 1863) 309-310.

"Lake Geneva Rhone…" Lyell, *Antiquity* 299-300.

"Labyrinthodon…" Sir Charles Lyell, *The Student's Elements of Geology*, 3rd edition (London: John Murray, 1878) 406.

"Archaeopteryx…" Lyell, *Antiquity* 450-452.

"Uncongenial climate…" Lyell, *Antiquity* 228.

"No human bones…" Lyell, *Antiquity* chapter 7.

"Virginia coal fields…" Lyell, *Elements of Geology* 372f.

"Fuller's earth…" Lyell, *Elements of Geology* 336.

"Age of copper lodes…" Lyell, *Elements* 617f.

"Veins of copper, lead…" Lyell, *Elements* 617.

"Scottish glacial drift…" Lyell, *Elements* 154.

"Pliocene strata…" Lyell, *Elements* 207.

"Central Asian loess…" Lyell, *Antiquity* note 35.

"Loam of Brixham caves… Lyell, *Elements* 113.

"An ecology…" Dave Wilkinson, "Ecology Before Ecology: Biogeography and Ecology in Lyell's 'Principles,'" *Journal of Biogeography,* 29 (2002) 1109-1115, DOI: 10.1046/j.1365-2699.2002.00754.x. Accessed December 30, 2017. Lyell's classic *Principles of Geology* was first published between 1830 and 1833 in three volumes.

"Neptunism or…" John W. Jade, *The Coming of Evolution: The Story of a Great Revolution in Science* (Cambridge: Cambridge University Press, 1910) 25. Neptunism is the old geological theory that rocks formed from mineral crystallization in the oceans, while Plutonism, expounded upon by geologist James Hutton and accepted and developed by Lyell, is the theory that the heat of the earth's interior explains the creation of certain kinds of rocks and of geological landscapes.

"Science and Bible…" Leonard G. Wilson, *Lyell in America: Transatlantic Geology, 1841-1853* (Baltimore: Johns Hopkins University Press, 1998) 2.

"Catastrophism…"
"Now Lyell…" Wilson, *Lyell in America* 1. Catastrophism is the theory that the earth's geology and crust formed through violent and unusual
events. Uniformitarianism, espoused by Lyell, is the theory that geological processes today are the same as, or similar to, processes in the past, "the present is key to the past."

"a catastrophic…" Wilson, *Lyell in America* 1.

"Humans weigh the stars..." Lyell, *Antiquity* 501.

"If humans were made…" Lyell, *Antiquity* 501.

"But to level us …" Lyell, *Antiquity* 502-504.

"Divine origin…" Lyell, *Antiquity* 505-506.
"Yet Linnaeus showed…" Lyell, *Antiquity* 474.

"Most all I have done…" Janet Browne, *Charles Darwin, The Power of Place* (Princeton: Princeton University Press, 2002) 417: "I never forget that almost everything which I have done in science I owe to the study of his great works." "I dreaded nothing so much as his surviving with impaired mental powers."

Section III

"thorough lessons…" Asa Gray, *Gray's School and Field Book of Botany* (New York: Ivison, Phinney, Blakeman & Co., 1869) 187.

"Learn from his passion…"
"his landmark research…" A. Hunter Dupree, *Asa Gray, American Botanist, Friend of*

Darwin. Baltimore, MD: Johns Hopkins University Press, 1988.

"but an advocate..." Browne, *The Power of Place* 216-217. Louis Agassiz, a famous and leading scientist of his day whose advancements are undeniable, has been criticized for his racial views, and thus his name has been removed from places that once honored him (although not Agassiz Peak, the second-tallest of the San Francisco Peaks at Flagstaff, AZ, where my daughter was born). On Agassiz and his work, see, for instance, Christoph Irmscher, "The Ambiguous Agassiz," *Humanities*, 34 (2013), https://www.neh.gov/humanities/2013/novemberdecember/feature/the-ambiguous-agassiz. Accessed December 21, 2017.

"like Agassiz's..." David Dobbs, "How Charles Darwin Seduced Asa Gray." Wired, April 28, 2011, https://www.wired.com/2011/04/how-charles-darwin-seduced-asa-gray/. Accessed August 29, 2017. Also, [Robert Chambers], *Vestiges of the Natural History of Creation. With a Sequel*. New York: Harper & Brothers [n.d.]. First published in 1844.

"Gray was convinced that..." Asa Gray, *Darwiniana: Essays and Reviews Pertaining to Darwinism* (New York: Appleton & Company. 1876) 369f, and 357f, 364f.

"religion. Look at..." Quoted in Lyell, *Antiquity* 506.

"But Darwin sought not..." Gray, *Darwiniana* 22.

"and he shed belief..." Darwin to Asa Gray, May 22 [1860], third paragraph. The quotation is: "Let each man hope & believe what he can." Darwin Correspondence Project, http://www.darwinproject.ac.uk/letter/DCP-LETT-2814.xml. Accessed December 17, 2017.

Section IV

"Wallace, explorer ..." A good biography of Wallace is Ross Slotten, *The Heretic in Darwin's Court: The Life of Alfred Russel Wallace*. New York: Columbia University Press, 2004.

"a major founder..."
"of flora, fauna..." The "Wallace Line" is the demarcation of flora and fauna of Asia and those of Australasia. Wallace first proposed the line (since revised) in 1859. See, for instance, Penny van Oosterzee, "Drawing the Line at Bali," ABC Science, http://www.abc.net.au/science/articles/2013/11/07/3885420.htm. Accessed January 12, 2018.

"Morning sun rises...." Alfred Russel Wallace, *The Malay Archipelago: The Land of the Orang-utan and the Bird of Paradise. A Narrative of Travel with Studies of Man and Nature* (London: Macmillan, 1890) 45-46.

"Islands of hot, moist..." Wallace, *Malay Archipelago* 1.

"*Ornithoptera*..."
"Bird of Paradise..." Oosterzee, "Drawing the Line at Bali."

"Huxley, Wallace..." Nizar Ibrahim and Ulrich Kutschera, "The Ornithologist Alfred Russe Wallace and the Controversy Surrounding the Dinosaurian Origin of Birds," *Theory in*

Biosciences, 4(2013) 267-75, DOI: 10.1007/s12064-013-0192-5. Accessed April 23, 2018.

"The three large islands..." Wallace, *Malay Archipelago* 109.

"Remarkable are ..." Wallace, *Malay Archipelago* 442-443.

"More diversity..." Alfred Russel Wallace, *Darwinism: An Exposition of the Theory of Natural Selection with Some of its Applications* (London: The Macmillan Co, 1896) 110.

"Animal structures..." Wallace, *Malay Archipelago* 205.

"Two native wolves..." Wallace, *Darwinism* 105.

"Titmice eat insects..." Wallace, *Darwinism* 107.

"Animals enjoy..." Wallace, *Darwinism* 37.

"The war of nature..."
"as they adapt..." Wallace, *Darwinism* 40 (quoting Darwin)

"How extinct species ..." Alfred Russel Wallace, "On the Law Which Has Regulated the Introduction of New Species" (1855), the section "Geologic Distinction of Forms of Life," and conclusion. Alfred Russel Wallace Classic Writings. Paper 2. The Alfred Russel Wallace Page, http://digitalcommons.wku.edu/dlps_fac_arw/2. Accessed December 14, 2017.

"Darwin, as he lay..." Unaware of Darwin's research (which he was still conducting for eventual publication), Wallace was suffering from a fever on the island of Halmahera in 1858 and, while ill, he had a sudden idea about natural selection as the mechanism of evolutionary development.

"and ideas from ..." Slotten, *Heretic* 28-31.

"*Vestiges*: species ..." Wallace, *Darwinism* 6.

"Agassiz: species ..." Wallace, *Darwinism* 5.

"selection, like a..."
"irregular traits..." Alfred Russel Wallace, "On the Tendency of Varieties to depart indefinitely from the Original Type," The Alfred Russel Wallace Page, http://people.wku.edu/charles.smith/essays/Wallace_On_the_Tendency_of_Varieties_to_Depart_Indefinitely_from_the_Original_Type.pdf. Accessed December 13, 2017.

"Darwin: females are..."
"Not so for Wallace..." Thierry Hoquet and Michael Levandowsky, "Utility vs Beauty: Darwin, Wallace and the Subsequent History of the Debate on Sexual Selection," in Thierry Hoquet and Michael Levandowsky, eds., *Current Perspectives on Sexual Selection. History, Philosophy and Theory of the Life Sciences*, 9 (2015), 19-44, doi.org/10.1007/978-94-017-9585-2_2. Accessed December 17, 2017. Also, Richard O. Prum, *The Evolution of Beauty:*

How Darwin's Forgotten Theory of Mate Choice Shapes the Animal World—and Us. New York: Doubleday, 2017.

"Wallace's vision…" Wallace's several books include *Tropical Life, and Other Essays* (1878), and *Man's Place in the Universe* (1904), in which he argued that life on other planets besides Earth is unlikely. Controversially, he was also interested in spiritualism.

"(At low stages…" Wallace, *Malay Archipelago* 456.

"Our English 'perfect'…" Wallace, *Malay Archipelago* 457.

Section V

"In 1950…" My copy of *The Origin of Species by Means of Natural Selection on the Preservation of Favored Races in the Struggle for Life* (London: John Murray, 1890) belonged to someone who underlined passages and circled a stain on page 248: "Celia's Suntan Lotion, Barranquilla, Columbia, 3-21-50."

"1858…" Randy Alfred, "July 1, 1858: Darwin and Wallace Shift the Paradigm," Wired, July 1, 2011, https://www.wired.com/2011/07/0701darwin-wallace-linnaean-society-london/. Accessed August 29, 2017.

"There is a struggle…"
"of each profitable…" Darwin, *Origin of Species* 404.

"life, governed by death…" Janet Browne, *Charles Darwin, Voyaging* (Princeton: Princeton University Press, 1995) 542-543. Browne writes: "… Darwin firmly drove the idea of God out of nature. As he was the first to recognize, his theory bleakly signaled the death of Adam" (p. 543), that is the "death" of modern *Homo sapiens* envisioned as created by God as complete and separate from other species.

"My new Pope couplet…" Alexander Pope's couplet "Epitaph for Sir Isaac Newton (Died March 21, 1727)" is: "NATURE and Nature's Laws lay hid in Night: God said, "Let Newton be!" and all was light."

"Huxley called himself…" Browne, *The Power of Place* 130

"Lyell, Huxley, Gray…"
"odd friends otherwise…" Browne, *The Power of Place* 130.

"the one living soul…" Darwin to J. D. Hooker, October 20, 1858. Darwin Correspondence Project. University of Cambridge, http://www.darwinproject.ac.uk/letter/DCP-LETT-2345.xml. Accessed Feb. 20, 2018.

"Darwin's ample beard…" Browne, *The Power of Place* 376.

"nor lend your name…" The official website of the Darwin Awards is darwinawards.com.

"If you hope to be..." Charles Darwin, *A Naturalist's Voyage: Journal of Researches into the Natural History and Geology of the Countries Visited during the Voyage of H.M.S. 'Beagle' Round the World under the Command of Capt. Fitzroy, R. N.* (London: John Murray, 1889) 509.

"Forty-seven shells..." Darwin, *A Naturalist's Voyage* 390-391.

"Amblyrhynelus ..." Darwin, *A Naturalist's Voyage* 385.

"Finch with cracking bills..." Darwin, *A Naturalist's Voyage* 379-381.

"'One might fancy that..."
"ago, one species..." Darwin, *A Naturalist's Voyage* 380.

"Not hopes, fears..." Charles Darwin, *The Descent of Man, and Selection in Relation to Sex* (New York: D. Appleton & Co., 1897) 619.

"As our planet spins..." Charles Darwin, *The Origin of Species* 429.

"I cannot endure..." Browne, *The Power of Place* 412.

"the forms and structures...." Charles Darwin, *The Structure and Distribution of Coral Reefs, Being the first part of the geology of the voyage of the Beagle, under the command of Capt. Fitzroy, R.N. during the years 1832 to 1836* (New York: D. Appleton & Co., 1897) 138.

"His work on orchids..."
"Life and letters (Vol. III, p. 274) quotes Asa Gray as saying that 'if the Orchid-book (with a few trifling omissions) had appeared before the "Origin" the author would have been canonised rather than anathematised by the natural theologians." From Darwin Online, *Fertilization of Orchids*, http://darwin-online.org.uk/EditorialIntroductions/Freeman_FertilisationofOrchids.html. Accessed November 30, 2017.

'Hermaphrodite plants..." Charles Darwin, *The Different Forms of Flowers on Plants of the Same Species* (New York: D. Appleton & Co., 1903) 344.

'More vigorous plants...." Browne, *The Power of Place* 414.

'Darwin feared..." Browne, *The Power of Place*, 423. Darwin was concerned about health problems among their children that might have resulted from his first-cousin marriage to Emma.

'Sexual selec-..."
the differences..." Darwin, *The Descent of Man* 605-606.

Wide-ranging thinker..." Browne, *The Power of Place* 182-183.

Darwin found daily..." Browne, *The Power of Place* 407.

"Darwin, Huxley watch…" Browne, *The Power of Place* 410.

"Insect murder!…" Browne, *The Power of Place* 409; Charles Darwin, *Insectivorous Plants.* London: John Murray, 1875.

"Infants, suffering…" Charles Darwin, *The Expression of the Emotions in Man and Animals* (London: John Murray, 1890) 155.

"Eyelids, firmly close…" Darwin, *Emotions* 155.

"Upper lip draw up…" Darwin, *Emotions* 155ff.

"Yet no tears are shed…" Darwin, *Emotions* 155, 161f.

"The insane may weep…" Darwin, *Emotions* 162.

"Elephants weep, too…" Darwin, *Emotions* 175f.

"Darwin: are inward…" Browne, *The Power of Place* 391.

"We personify…" Darwin, *Origin of Species* 63.

"but need not claim…" Darwin, *Origin of Species* 62-64.

"We expose living…" Darwin, *Origin of Species* 62-64.

"The law of Lamarck…" Darwin, *Origin of Species* xiv.

"but 'Pangenesis'…" Charles Darwin, *The Variation of Animals and Plants under Domestication,* Vol. 2 (London: John Murray, 1882) chapter 27.

"Thanks to Mendel…" William Bateson, *Mendel's Principles of Heredity* (Cambridge Cambridge University press, 1909) 288.

"Transmutation: no…" Bateson, *Mendel's Principles* 288ff.

"Spencer's classic phrase…" Charles Darwin, *The Variation of Animals and Plants under Domestication*, Vol. 1 (London: John Murray, 1882) 6. Philosopher, biologist, sociologist Herbert Spencer coined the phrase "survival of the fittest" in his 1864 book *Principles of Biology.* Darwin used the phrase in his *Animals and Plants* book (first published in 1868) and added the phrase to the fifth edition of *On the Origin of Species* in 1869.

"nor only fitness…"
"and groups expand…"
"Species transmutate…" See, for instance, articles cited at the Wikipedia article "Survival of the Fittest" (accessed Nov. 24, 2017), such as Sarda Sahney, Michael J. Benton, Paul A. Ferr "Links between global taxonomic diversity, ecological diversity and the expansion of vertebrates on land" (2010), *Biology Letters,* 6(4) (2010): 544–547, DOI: 10.1098

rsbl.2009.1024. Accessed November 24, 2017. Also Momme von Sydow, 'Survival of the Fittest' in "Darwinian Metaphysics - Tautology or Testable Theory?" (2014) 199-222, in Eckart Voigts, Barbara Schaff, and Monika Pietrzak-Franger, eds, *Reflecting on Darwin* (London: Ashgate, 2014), http://crisp.psi.uni-heidelberg.de/sites/default/files/vonSydow/von_Sydow_2014_Survival_of_the_Fittest_in_Darwinian_Metaphysics_Scan.pdf. Accessed November 24, 2017.

"Fisher, Haldane, Wright..." See the Wikipedia article sources on "Modern Synthesis (20th Century"), https://en.wikipedia.org/wiki/Modern_synthesis_(20th_century). Accessed December 13, 2017. See especially Arlin Stoltzfus, "Mendelian-Mutationism: The Forgotten Evolutionary Synthesis," *Journal of the History of Biology* 47 (2014), 501–546, DOI 10.1007/s10739-014-9383-2. Accessed December 13, 2017.

Section VI

"*Origin*, published.."
"No more belief that..."
"wrong hypothesis..." Randall Fuller, *The Book That Changed America: How Darwin's Theory of Evolution Ignited a Nation*. New York: Viking Press, 2017.

"Lincoln the lawyer..." For Darwin's hatred of slavery, see *A Naturalist's Voyage* 499-500.

"Who'd have thought Lincoln..." Lincoln and Darwin were both born on February 12, 1809.

"As much as Stonewall's..." Daniel W. Stowell, "Stonewall Jackson and the Providence of God," chapter 8 of Randall M. Miller, Harry S. Stout, Charles Reagan Wilson, eds., *Religion and the American Civil War* (Oxford: Oxford University Press, 1998) 187-207.

"ten tons of dry earth... Charles Darwin, *The Formation of Vegetable Mould through the Action of Worms, with Observations on their Habits* (London, John Murray, 1882) 308.

"Worm castings..." Darwin, *Formation of Vegetable Mould* 309.

"Earth is reborn..." Adam Phillips, *Darwin's Worms* (New York: Basic Books, 2000) 58: "It is as though the earth is reborn again and again, passing through the bodies of worms. Darwin has replaced a creation myth with a secular maintenance myth."

"Church fathers demand..." Andrew Dickson White, *A History of the Warfare of Science with Theology in Christendom*, Vol. 1 (New York: D. Appleton & Co., 1897) 25.

'Could not the Holy..." Suggested by Rev. Samuel Kinns, *Moses and Geology; or, The Harmony of the Bible with Science*. London: Cassell & Co., 1887.

"Creation happened..." The 17th century Archbishop of Armagh, James Ussher, calculated the creation of the earth as happening in 4004 BCE, based on Old Testament chronology and other sources.

Although several other scholars developed similar calculations, using similar methodology accepted in their time, Ussher's chronology began to be included in Bible translations and thus took on an almost scriptural authority.

"Euclid's figures..." Kinns, *Moses and Geology* 355-356.

"Huxley coined the word..." Thomas Huxley, *Christianity and Agnosticism: A Controversy. II. Agnosticism* (NY: The Humboldt Publishing Co., 1889), https://archive.org/stream/agnosticism00variuoft/agnosticism00variuoft_djvu.txt. Accessed December 20, 2017. "Agnosticism, in fact, is not a creed, but a method, the essence of which lies in the rigorous application of a single principle... the fundamental axiom of modern science... In matters of the intellect, follow your reason as far as it will take you, without regard to any other consideration..."

"Why do you complain..."
"and Pythagorus...." Judd, *The Coming of Evolution* 3

"Bible, not Darwin..." Kinns, *Moses and Geology* 356.

"Beloved is man..." Judah Goldin, ed., *The Living Talmud: The Wisdom of the Fathers and Its Classical Commentaries* (New York: The Heritage Press, 1957) 77. Translation of the Mishnah tractate *Pirkei Avot.*

"The *Pirkei Avot...*" *Living Talmud* 113.

"Ten generations..." *Living Talmud* 114.

"All were created..."
"Scripture, by the First..." *Living Talmud* 121-122.

"The Sages: study ..." *Living Talmud* 114.

"Take Psalm...." J. Clinton McCann, Jr., "The Book of Psalms," in *The New Interpreter's Bible*, Vol. IV (Nashville: Abingdon Press, 1996) 1099-1100: "In a profound sense, Psalm 104 puts us humans in our place—with springs and hills and trees and creating things. If our motivation for facing our own future and the future of the earth were to glorify God, we might even have the humility to ask ourselves what it would really mean to live in partnership with a tree or with a wild goat or with the thousands of species whose disappearance causes hardly a ripple of attention, primarily because we are convinced the nature exists to serve humanity. Quite simply, Psalm 104 asserts that this is not the case. Rather, to serve God will mean ultimately to serve God's creation..." (p. 1100).

"birds and beasts and ...." Psalm 104:24-25.

"Human being: no..." Malcolm Jeeves, ed., *From Cells to Souls-And Beyond: Changing Portraits of Human Nature* (Grand Rapids: Eerdmans, 2004) 194, 196. *Nephesh* is a Hebrew word from the Bible meaning "soul" or "life" or "sentient being."

"Spiritual truth..." 1 Corinthians 15:51-52.

"(Faith's other side..." Richard Dawkins, quoted in "Has the world changed?—Part two," *The Guardian*, October 11, 2011, https://www.theguardian.com/world/2001/oct/11/afghanistan.terrorism2. Accessed December 23, 2017. Dawkins writes, "Revealed faith is not harmless nonsense, it can be lethally dangerous nonsense... Dangerous because it teaches enmity to others labelled only by a difference of inherited tradition."

"Wise the preacher..." A New England minister, William Wisner Adams, preached an annual sermon about recent astronomical discoveries. He is said to have explained that such discoveries broadened his view of God. Peter Gomes, *The Good Book: Reading the Bible with Mind and Heart* (San Francisco: HarperSanFrancisco, 1996) 312, cited in Paul E. Stroble, *What About Religion and Science? A Study of Reason and Faith* (Nashville: Abingdon Press, 2007) 78.

"Again, Darwin's praise..."
"endless forms..." Darwin, *Origin of Species* 429.

"Religion, science..." See Stephen Jay Gould, *Rocks of Ages: Science and Religion in the Fullness of Life*. New York: Ballantine Books, 1999. Gould proposed that science and religion represent "non-overlapping magisteria," that is, legitimate domains of inquiry that do not overlap and thus do not need to conflict.

Section VII

"Consider life..." Browne, *The Power of Place* 373.

"Charles and wife Emma..." Browne, *The Power of Place* 401.

"Ralph Vaughan Williams..." Charles Lyell is also buried in Westminster Abbey, as is Isaac Newton. Memorial tablets at the Abbey honor Wallace and Hooker.

"Happy is the one..." Proverbs 3:13, sung by the choir at Darwin's funeral: Browne, *The Power of Place* 497. For the first line, I changed "man" to "one".

Paul Stroble teaches at Webster University in St. Louis and Eden Theological Seminary. A native of Vandalia, Illinois, he lives in St. Louis. A grantee of the National Endowment for the Humanities and the Louisville Institute, he has written twenty-one books and numerous articles, essays, and curricular materials. Finishing Line Press has published his three other chapbooks: *Dreaming at the Electric Hobo* (2015), *Little River* (2017), and *Small Corner of the Stars* (2017).

CPSIA information can be obtained
at www.ICGtesting.com
Printed in the USA
LVHW091002110119
603520LV00001B/79/P